The Duties and Responsibilities of
the Secretary of Defense

David C. Ruffin

The Rosen Publishing Group's
PowerKids Press™
New York

Dedicated to my father, David C. Ruffin Jr.,
who served in the United States Navy during World War II

Published in 2005 by The Rosen Publishing Group, Inc.
29 East 21st Street, New York, NY 10010

Copyright © 2005 by The Rosen Publishing Group, Inc.

First Edition

Editor: Frances E. Ruffin
Book Design: Albert B. Hanner
Photo Researcher: Sherri Liberman

Photo Credits: Cover, pp. 4, 19, 20, 28 © AP/Wide World Photo; p. 7 Doug Mills/AP Photo p. 8 (left) © Scala/Art Resource, NY; p. 8 (left) © Scala/Art Resource, (right) © Hulton/Archive/Getty Images; pp. 11, 12 (top and bottom) © Bettmann/CORBIS; pp. 15 (top), 27 (bottom) © AFP/CORBIS; p. 15 (bottom) Defense Visual Information Center, March ARB, CA.; p. 16 © Lee Jae-Won/Reuters/CORBIS; p. 23 U.S. Air Force Photo by Airman 1st Class Alicia Sarkkinen; p. 24 U.S. Naval Academy; p. 27 (top) © Peter Turnley/CORBIS.

Library of Congress Cataloging-in-Publication Data

Ruffin, David C.
   The duties and responsibilities of the Secretary of Defense /
David C. Ruffin.
      p. cm. — (Your government in action)
   Includes bibliographical references and index.
   ISBN 1-4042-2689-3 (Library Binding)
   1. United States. Dept. of Defense—History—Juvenile literature. [1. United States. Dept. of Defense. Office of the Secretary of Defense. 2. United States. Dept. of Defense—History.] I. Title. II. Series: Ruffin, David C. Your government in action.
UA23.6.R84 2005
355'.00973—dc22

2003024462

Manufactured in the United States of America

Contents

Here F-16 Falcon jet fighters patrol the skies. Pilots in the U.S. Air Force fly these planes to help defend America.

The Secretary of Defense Protects Americans

The U.S. secretary of defense helps to protect America. One of the secretary's duties is to look for ways to prevent terrorist attacks from other countries. Terrorists are people who believe that causing harm is the only way to get what they want. Another part of the job is to find and punish terrorists who harm America.

On September 11, 2001, terrorists from other countries flew airplanes into the two World Trade Center towers in New York City. The planes exploded and destroyed the buildings. Terrorists also flew a plane into the Pentagon, which is the headquarters for the U.S. Department of Defense. The building is located in Virginia near Washington, D.C. About 3,000 people were killed by these attacks. Donald Rumsfeld was the secretary of defense at the time the attacks occurred.

The Leader of America's Military

Under the American system of government, the U.S. president is the commander in chief of all American fighting men and women. However, the president gives the secretary of defense the authority to protect the United States from any group outside the United States that might try to harm Americans. The secretary of defense is the leader of the Department of Defense. This department includes the Army, Navy, Air Force, and Marines. These are the four branches of the U.S. Armed Forces, or the military. The secretary's office is in the Pentagon. It is the secretary's job to make sure that America's armed forces are well trained. The secretary must also see to it that men and women in the military have the weapons, uniforms, food, and **equipment** they need to do their jobs well.

Mexico's defense secretary General Gerardo Clemente Ricardo Vega Garcia, right, and U.S. defense secretary Donald H. Rumsfeld, left, review troops during an armed forces full honor ceremony for Garcia at the Pentagon.

The seal of the Defense Department shows the eagle in its center. The eagle represents the United States and strength.

Men fight the British at the Battle of Bunker Hill in 1775. This was one of the first battles of the American Revolution.

Henry Knox, the first ▶ secretary of war, lived from 1750 to 1806 and fought during the American Revolution.

America's First Military Leaders

From the time the United States became a nation, it has needed protection from its enemies. In 1783, the United States won the **American Revolution** against Great Britain. Four years later, the 13 states agreed to be **united** under the U.S. **Constitution**. The Constitution made the president the commander in chief of the Army and the Navy. In 1789, George Washington was elected the first U.S. president. He selected other men to advise him and help him run the government. These advisers were called the cabinet. A secretary of war was made part of the cabinet to make sure that the United States had a strong army. In 1798, a secretary of the navy was added to the cabinet. For 149 years, the secretary of war and secretary of the navy shared the job of protecting the United States.

Henry Knox became the first secretary of war. Benjamin Stoddert was the first secretary of the navy.

The First Secretary of Defense

In 1947, President Harry S. Truman appointed James Forrestal to be the first secretary of defense. He became the secretary of defense at a **dangerous** time. **Communist** countries, such as the Union of Soviet Socialist Republics (U.S.S.R.) and China, were trying to conquer weaker countries. In Communist countries citizens do not have the right of free speech or the right to vote for their leaders. By 1949, the U.S.S.R. also had learned how to make **atomic bombs**. Forrestal began to build up military bases in European countries that were threatened by the U.S.S.R. James Forrestal's most valuable contribution was to make the U.S. Armed Forces stronger by joining the military. The Army, Navy, and Air Force became one team under the Department of Defense.

James Forrestal was America's first secretary of defense. Before James Forrestal was named secretary of defense, he had been a businessman and the secretary of the navy.

MEDIUM RANGE BALLISTIC MISSILE BASE IN CUBA
SAN CRISTOBAL

LAUNCH POSITION
MISSILE-READY TENTS
MISSILE ERECTORS
LATE OCTOBER

Secretary of Defense Robert McNamara points to a map of Vietnam in August 1964. He tells the public that the Navy is attacking North Vietnam.

The Defense Department took pictures of a missile base in San Cristobal, Cuba, in October 1962.

Missiles in Cuba

Robert McNamara became secretary of defense in 1961, under President John F. Kennedy. From 1961 to 1968, Robert McNamara added 1,000,000 men and women to the U.S. Armed Forces. About 500,000 Americans fought against Communist armies in the Vietnam War. In 1962, the U.S.S.R. put **missiles** in Cuba. This island in the Caribbean Sea is 90 miles (145 km) from the United States. Those missiles could reach American cities and destroy them. Secretary McNamara helped President Kennedy decide to stop ships coming from the U.S.S.R. to Cuba. This blockade worked. The missiles were sent back to the U.S.S.R. and the United States did not have to go to war.

Before he became the secretary of defense in 1961, Robert McNamara was the president of the Ford Motor Company, which makes cars and trucks.

Soap, Planes, and Gasoline

Today in the Department of Defense, there are about 1,400,000 men and women who are serving in the military full-time. About 1,200,000 part-time members serve in the National Guard or its reserves. The national guard and reserves can be called upon to fight in an **emergency**.

The defense secretary has other people who help him run the Department of Defense. Some of these people head the **agencies** and organizations in the Department of Defense that do special jobs. For example, the U.S. **Transportation** Command has ships and planes that can move an entire army to the other side of the world. Another department buys the things the Armed Forces need, such as trucks, blankets, bullets, soap, gasoline, and food. Also reporting to the secretary of defense are secretaries of the Army, the Navy, and the Air Force.

The Department of Defense is always looking for new and better ways to protect the United States. The X-45 Unmanned Combat Air Vehicle is an experimental pilotless jet fighter. It will collect facts as well as be an attack plane that will help save soldiers' lives.

Supplies are being gathered at this military supply point in California. They will be used by marines who are fighting in the 2003 Operation Enduring Freedom to help people in Afghanistan.

The Army

The secretary of the army works for the defense secretary. This person heads the department responsible for fighting on the ground. Many Army soldiers are placed in divisions of between 15,000 and 18,000 men and women. There are different kinds of divisions. Armored divisions use tanks and other ground **vehicles**. **Infantry** divisions fight with rifles and weapons that the soldiers can carry themselves. One hundred and fifty years ago, soldiers fought on foot or on horseback. Today soldiers go into battle in trucks, helicopters, or vehicles that have thick steel armor that can stop bullets. Army **paratroopers** jump out of airplanes from 800 feet (244 m) and float to the ground in **parachutes**.

An Army Abrams tank weighs 160,000 pounds (72,579 kg). That is about the weight of 45 cars put together.

◄ *This Army soldier explains the Javelin Anti-tank Missile to another soldier during a training exercise in 2002. This missile is used to stop tanks.*

The Navy

The secretary of the navy also works for the secretary of defense. He or she heads a department of sailors and marines. The main job of the Navy is to keep the world's oceans free of enemy vessels. This way all ships can travel on them. The Navy has to be able to fight in faraway places. The Navy uses many different kinds of ships. For example, aircraft carriers are huge ships that carry between 85 and 100 jet planes. During a war, an aircraft carrier sails to an area near the battle so its airplanes can attack ships or enemies on land. The Navy also has **submarines** that can **launch** Trident missiles that can hit enemies as far as 7,000 miles (11,300 km) away. Sailors can stay underwater in their submarines for nearly 100 days without coming to the surface.

Sailors in the Navy stand on the decks of aircraft carrier USS Abraham Lincoln *as they arrive in San Diego harbor. The carrier had been at sea for 10 months and the sailors were part of the fighting in Iraq.*

The Marines

The marines are part of the Navy. They are headed by the secretary of the navy, who reports to the secretary of defense. Marines can be called seagoing soldiers because they move on ships, but mostly they fight on the ground the way soldiers do. In a war, marines are often the first to fight. Marines are carried by helicopters or special boats that float over the water on a cushion of air at 40 miles per hour (64 km/h). Being a good rifleman who can work with a team is the most important part of being a marine. Marines have to be ready to fight anywhere. They may fight in a jungle, in a desert, or among cold mountain peaks. Marines and other members of the Armed Forces wear special **camouflage** clothes in battle so they can blend into their surroundings.

Marines take part in a training exercise in Manila, in the Philippines. Seven hundred U.S. marines and 700 Philippine marines worked together in the exercise.

The Air Force

The secretary of the air force reports to the secretary of defense. He or she heads a department whose job is to keep the skies safe. The Air Force has jet fighter planes with cannons and missiles that can fight other planes in the air. There are also bombers that can attack enemies on the ground. The Air Force has planes that carry soldiers with their weapons, equipment, food, and vehicles for long distances to battlefields. The Air Force also has powerful missiles that can attack an enemy that is 5,000 miles (8,046 km) away. Many Air Force planes can fly thousands of miles (km) without landing because they are refueled in the air from large tanker airplanes.

Staff Sergeant Eugenia Lopez of the U.S. Air Force checks the equipment in the central radar control office in Iraq. She is one of the people who is ▶ responsible for controlling all air traffic in Iraq.

Training Men and Women to Fight

A very important job for the secretary of defense is to make sure that members of the Armed Forces receive proper training in hundreds of schools. As part of this job, the Defense Department runs the U.S. Military Academy at West Point, New York, the U.S. Naval Academy at Annapolis, Maryland, and the U.S. Air Force Academy at Colorado Springs, Colorado.

All members of the armed forces receive at least six weeks of basic training. After basic training, they can attend schools that provide training for jobs such as missile specialists, pilots, engine mechanics, radio operators, animal care specialists, and cooks.

Donald Rumsfeld is the only person to be appointed secretary of defense twice. The first time he was the youngest defense secretary in history. The second time he was the oldest.

During basic training, young men and women are taught military customs, such as how to march and what will be expected of them during their military service. Here cadets graduate from the Naval Academy.

Defending People Around the World

The most important job of the secretary of defense is to make the United States strong so that its enemies are afraid to attack. Defense secretaries are in charge of all the people who serve on American military bases worldwide. They provide defense and leadership for America's allies, or friends. For example, George C. Marshall was Harry S. Truman's defense secretary when the United States led United Nations forces against North Korea. They wanted to keep it from conquering South Korea.

In 1990, Iraqi president Saddam Hussein's army took control of oil fields in nearby Kuwait. In 1991, Secretary of Defense Richard Cheney ordered American forces to remove the Iraqi army from Kuwait. This conflict was called the Persian Gulf War. The secretary of defense protects not only Americans, but also our allies around the world.

These soldiers march through the Saudi Arabian desert during the Persian Gulf War. Successful American forces conquered the Iraqi army.

Secretary of Defense William S. Cohen speaks with Congress to ask them to approve additional spending in Kosovo. The U.S. Armed Forces entered Kosovo to put a stop to what was happening there. Certain groups were being killed for their beliefs.

Secretaries of Defense from 1947 to 2005

James V. Forrestal, 1947–1949
Louis A. Johnson, 1949–1950
George C. Marshall, 1950–1951
Robert A. Lovett, 1951–1953
Charles E. Wilson, 1953–1957
Neil H. McElroy, 1957–1959
Thomas S. Gates, 1959–1961
Robert S. McNamara, 1961–1968
Clark M. Clifford, 1968–1969
Melvin R. Laird, 1969–1973
Elliot L. Richardson, 1973

James R. Schlesinger, 1973–1975
Donald H. Rumsfeld, 1975–1977
Harold Brown, 1977–1981
Casper W. Weinberger, 1981–1987
Frank C. Carlucci, 1987–1989
Richard B. Cheney, 1989–1993
Les Aspin, 1993–1994
William J. Perry, 1994–1997
William S. Cohen, 1997–2001
Donald H. Rumsfeld, 2001–

◀ *The Pentagon in Washington, D.C., is the headquarters of the Department of Defense. The five-sided building houses 23,000 employees who work to keep America safe.*

The secretary of Defense has many duties and responsibilities. The thousands of people who assist the secretary work in the agencies of the Defense Department that are outlined in this chart.

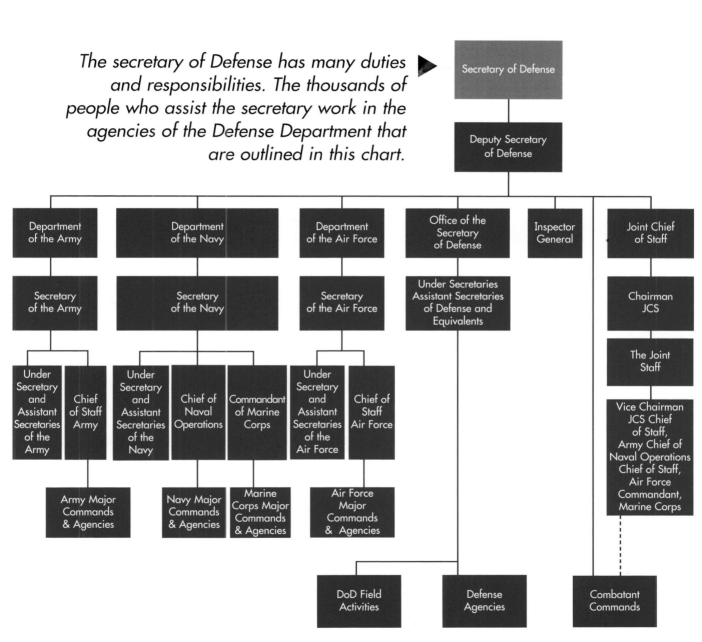

Secretary of Defense

Deputy Secretary of Defense

Department of the Army
Department of the Navy
Department of the Air Force
Office of the Secretary of Defense
Inspector General
Joint Chief of Staff

Secretary of the Army
Secretary of the Navy
Secretary of the Air Force
Under Secretaries Assistant Secretaries of Defense and Equivalents
Chairman JCS

Under Secretary and Assistant Secretaries of the Army
Chief of Staff Army
Under Secretary and Assistant Secretaries of the Navy
Chief of Naval Operations
Commandant of Marine Corps
Under Secretary and Assistant Secretaries of the Air Force
Chief of Staff Air Force
The Joint Staff

Army Major Commands & Agencies
Navy Major Commands & Agencies
Marine Corps Major Commands & Agencies
Air Force Major Commands & Agencies
Vice Chairman JCS Chief of Staff, Army Chief of Naval Operations Chief of Staff, Air Force Commandant, Marine Corps

DoD Field Activities
Defense Agencies
Combatant Commands

Timeline

1775	The Continental Congress asks George Washington to become general and commander in chief of the Continental army.
1785	George Washington selects Henry Knox to become the first secretary of war.
1789	Washington adds a secretary of war to his cabinet.
1941	Ground is broken in Arlington, Virginia, to build the Pentagon, the headquarters of the department of war.
1943	The Pentagon, a five-sided building, and one of the largest office buildings in the world, is completed. Today, as the headquarters of the Department of Defense, it houses about 23,000 employees.
1945	President Harry S. Truman makes plans to create a department of defense.
1947	Former secretary of the navy James V. Forrestal becomes the first secretary of defense.
1990–1991	More than 250,000 soldiers, including 40,000 women, are sent to the Middle East in Operations Desert Shield and Desert Storm.
2001	On September 11, terrorists take over airplanes by force and crash them into targets that include the Pentagon.
2003	The United States sends troops to Iraq as part of the War on Terror.

Glossary

agencies (A-jen-seez) Special departments of the government.

American Revolution (uh-MER-uh-ken reh-vuh-LOO-shun) Battles that soldiers from the colonies fought against Britain for freedom, from 1775 to 1783.

atomic bombs (uh-TAH-mik BAHMZ) Powerful explosives that produce great force, heat, and a blinding light.

camouflage (KA-muh-flaj) To hide by using a color and a pattern that matches one's surroundings.

Communist (KOM-yuh-nist) Belonging to a system in which all the land, houses, and factories belong to the government and are shared by everyone.

Constitution (kon-stih-TOO-shun) The basic rules by which the United States is governed.

dangerous (DAYN-jer-us) Able to cause harm.

emergency (ih-MUR-jin-see) An event that happens in which quick help is needed.

equipment (uh-KWIP-mint) All the supplies needed to do an activity.

infantry (IN-fun-tree) The part of an army that fights on foot.

launch (LONCH) To push out or to put into the air.

missiles (MIH-sulz) Rockets used to put things such as weapons into the air.

parachutes (PAR-uh-shoots) Large pieces of cloth shaped like umbrellas that are used in jumping safely from an aircraft.

paratroopers (PAR-uh-troop-erz) Soldiers who are trained to jump out of airplanes.

submarines (SUB-muh-reenz) Ships that are made to travel underwater.

transportation (tranz-per-TAY-shun) A way of traveling from one place to another.

united (yoo-NYT-ed) Brought together to act as a single group.

vehicles (VEE-uh-kulz) Means of moving or carrying things.

Index

Web Sites

Due to the changing nature of Internet links, PowerKids Press has developed an online list of Web sites related to the subject of this book. This site is updated regularly. Please use this link to access the list:
www.powerkidslinks.com/yga/drsd/